PRAISE FOR WRONSKY'S PREVIOUS WORK

"Difficult and rewarding, like H.D.'s work . . . smart, classy poems . . . "
—*Library Journal*

"The diction and observations come together seamlessly, showing us our (gendered) vulnerabilities . . ."
—*Publishers Weekly*

"Rhythmic urgency and a faultless, inventive music . . ."
—*The Boston Review*

"Wronsky writes about the world she sees with endless compassion and deft perception."
—*Culture Trip*

"Gail Wronsky, an acclaimed poet, has somehow given birth to a completely new form . . ."
—*Los Angeles Times Book Review*

LOS ANGELES

ALSO BY GAIL WRONSKY

Dogland (chapbook)
Again the Gemini are in the Orchard
Dying for Beauty
The Love-Talkers
Poems for Infidels
Blue Shadow Behind Everything Dazzling (chapbook)
Bling & Fringe (with Molly Bendall)
So Quick Bright Things
Tomorrow You'll be One of Us (with Chuck Rosenthal)

TRANSLATIONS
Volando Bajito by Alicia Partnoy
Fuegos Florales by Alicia Partnoy

IMPERFECT PASTORALS

GAIL WRONSKY

LOS ANGELES

Copyright © 2017 by Gail Wronsky. All rights reserved. Published in the United States by What Books Press, the imprint of the Glass Table Collective, Los Angeles.

Publisher's Cataloging-In-Publication Data

Names: Wronsky, Gail.
Title: Imperfect pastorals / Gail Wronsky.
Description: Los Angeles : What Books Press, [2017]
Identifiers: ISBN 978-1-5323-4139-7
Subjects: LCSH: Los Angeles (Calif.)--Poetry. | Pastoral poetry, American.
Classification: LCC PS3623.R66 I46 2017 | DDC 811/.6--dc23

Cover art: Gronk, *Past Imperfection*, mixed media on paper, 2016
Book design by Ash Good, www.ashgood.design

What Books Press
363 South Topanga Canyon Boulevard
Topanga, CA 90290

WHATBOOKSPRESS.COM

IMPERFECT PASTORALS

For Chuck, always

CONTENTS

Clearer than amber gliding over stones	13
The light and shade upon the globe	14
For not in vain we name the constellations	15
What delays the long nights	16
Dry cracking sounds are heard	17
An acre or two of land that no one wanted	19
Praise large estates, but cultivate a small one	20
So much effect has habit on the young	21
And mend the wreckage of a ruined home	22
Wild beasts and fish, cattle and colored birds	23
Alone, rather because not otherwise	24
Leading the solemn procession joyfully	25
By some strange gladness elated	26
Led by these signs and by these instances	27
Flame-color means east winds	28
The heron leaves her haunt in the marsh	29
Headlong falls the sky in sheets of rain	30
Work at your ominous evensong in vain	31
Against the dark, long trails of luminous white	32
If once that well-known scent comes down the wind	33
An ant that fears a lean old age	34
And in green meadows raise a marble temple	35
In temples ivories wept and bronzes sweated	36
His eyes ablaze with sea-green light	37
Light chaff and falling leaves or a pair of feathers	38

Drawn by a team of three-legged fish-tailed horses	40
Days such as these shone out and went their way	42
Let not the spangled lizard's scaly back	44
in these latitudes/of indeterminate/waves	46
Pitch-pines or guilty yews or dark green ivy	47
Through the liquid air of summer	49
New treatments made things worse	50
Wild olives, bitter-leaved, alone survive	52
Let thought become your beautiful lover	53
What is it that slows the lingering dusk	54
And the wild willow-bed demands attention	55
How lucky, if they know their happiness	56
Dolphins are People Too	57
Miraculously pregnant by the wind	59
Even girls spinning their nightly stint of wool	60
Kamikaze Feminist Fish	62
Far be it from me to indulge in a nap	63
Then are wild thickets loud with singing birds	64
What need to tell of autumn's storms and stars	65
Selectively, using your fingernails	66
The trees that lift themselves spontaneously	67
Or rain of acorns from a shaken oak	68
When it's bone-hard under a north wind	69
The bank all green with celery, the cucumber snaking	70
A spacious cave much visited by waves	71
We offer reeking entrails to the gods	72
And the owl on the rooftop watching the sun go down	73
Notes and Acknowledgments	74

" . . . our creative/Winged seed can strike a root in anything."
—C. Day Lewis

CLEARER THAN AMBER
GLIDING OVER STONES

is the sunlight of thought. Quieter than the crisp fiction of windlessness—
Production, consumption—

are you tired of convincing people you're not trying to convince them of
anything?
I am. Soil is necessary. Perhaps we could agree on that—

and stop cupping our hands beneath dry sky as if we knew what we wanted.
A name for what it is that happens in our minds when we're ecstatic and
alone. When

briefly destiny uncries, like someone in a movie weeping backward.
Perhaps nothing can trump the rose of this mind-thriving (not even

the final, sealing hush of golden Buddha).
Maybe we're trapped innately, gnat-like, in the middle of great vacant signs.

Maybe we just think we are.

THE LIGHT AND SHADE
UPON THE GLOBE

World or thought—which of the two thinks the other?

I think too much at the risk of seducing myself and

sashaying away through the topiary aviary of

life. What thinkst thou? That the earth is small

and blue, that doors and windows open onto ether and

death, that you'd go all the way to the moon and back

for a breakfast of fondue de poireaux and Absolut.

We're veiling our statues this morning so that whatever

music there is can be unabashed. We're garlanding an entrance

to the future—a portal—a mirrored tortoise shell. Now

we're thinking again! Thinking we can sustain the

whole planet with our moods. When only you can.

FOR NOT IN VAIN WE NAME THE CONSTELLATIONS

Distracted, I too wandered as far as the pont Louis-Phillippe.
The winking of the stars I understood--metallic exceptions

and irritations, then the dawn of eyes and eyeing--of spilled
wine leaking into the mouth of the earth, or is it an ear

into which I can shout, scattering the names of my ancestors

all the way to wherever? Emptying temples, the day turning
this way then that. Coffee with the poet who says, "I'm a fake.

A total fraud." Then dinner with the climatologist. I'm not
saying all of this is or isn't meaningful—it's just that I prefer

certain things to remain anonymous—unlike the bears circling
the illuminated Paris skyline. Or the swan soaring above its own

four-pointed reflection. Or the Seine weeping incoherently
but in French.

WHAT DELAYS THE LONG NIGHTS

Slumped au naturel in a rattan chair,
awash in the desert of my faithfulness . . .

Doors provide unexpected openings.
Windows, when not false, open "in

praise of the new polemic," producing
the desired effect of estrangement. Under

the circumstances, oppressed by desire, I
open a can of fish, if not worms, if not

dismembered mermaids; I kiss the bloom
of a captive orchid enigmatic as weeping

and as echo. A black cat moves from room
to room. I remember the time my lover,

Aeolis, took on the raucous, rolling body
of an autumn storm . . .

DRY CRACKING SOUNDS
ARE HEARD

The path ahead   glitters in dialectic.

Why do we feel instinctual--
     motley-clad?
                             It
    overwhelms logic.

We think answers
     can be found by pressing

against boundaries   yes so we press
        against beliefs, for

example, the philosophical given
that a thing   can only be true if it is

as beautiful as nature.
(Aristotle's reverence for natural beauty

was it based on
adoration or acquisition?   This is

something I'd
       like to know, as if
    the difference is more
       significant than the similarity
between

the two). Don't you love other people's
        shimmering
bits of thought—

walking through   words like a
        happy
and avaricious   zombie

clown—
                (totally non-hierarchical)?

AN ACRE OR TWO OF LAND
THAT NO ONE WANTED

Let me stress once again, says Baudrillard,
that it is not the fragility of objects that
is tragic, nor their death. Rather it is the
temptation represented by that fragility
and that death

    —the temptation to annihilate

which we confront by not confronting things,

letting them go to seed, to pot, to hell, to waste, a fate which is
                in some ways worse than death. And they respond to our neglect,

our oftentimes casual dismissal, by rising up against us in their quiet ways,

which could be why each time I drive past a certain
        uninhabited property on the warehouse road I find myself
thinking we were born for no reason but to die and be forgotten. It's what

the exhausted machinery there wishes to have me believe.

I'd make a counter-argument, except that I was born
        for no reason; I will die and be forgotten. So it all seems rather
                moot.

PRAISE LARGE ESTATES, BUT CULTIVATE A SMALL ONE

Let's not be awed.　　　Keep focus

on want's　　very meager　expectancy.　　Hope not.

You want to write　　　a poem in the sky?　I

　want it to　　　say　　　Only If

We Let Them　　　　Take Us　　Apart

Will We　　　Die. But　　the day　　　goes by

and the　　　miserly　　eternal　　　tries to snatch it

awry,　　　leaving a puffy　　　Rorschach for

the beach-goers.　　　A shy

woman really, my　　　tongue　　clings

to the roof of my　　mouth.　　　Clings to the quick

of all　　talking.　　　It's a trap, the praise song.　We

finish　　　in the diminutive.

SO MUCH EFFECT HAS HABIT ON THE YOUNG

To each   her lair of solitude   the blur

and   spidery confines of being

(hovering personages   notwithstanding)

she wants engagement in the fungible aspects

of play   wants to play with

some ur-word   a contingently configured

field of   potential on the page

(but oh my daughter there's nothing but water)

so she goes it solo   from the stony bottom

of the well   of solipsism   reading

as when we were children   and our

books broke   apart   in the infinite

breaking   of all words   and the hillsides

grew   crazy radiant   in confetti and

(the birds of the air filled her heart with despair)

AND MEND THE WRECKAGE
OF A RUINED HOME

laughter   as when

      alone at night   reading aloud

the sea, the clacking sound of oars   the first

      cutting of the thumbnail with a razor

      it wasn't so much after all to lose

as when   losing

      there was music   but it's   breaking

up amid the   mending   all

      bruised and buried   under a once

bright   winter sun

   we're   done now

      as ashy as   decimated cinder blocks

we hate to/have to

batter the door   this way

WILD BEASTS AND FISH, CATTLE AND COLORED BIRDS

I would not have lain in the grave of this body so long

were it not for the enticements of animal   life

were it not for tigers   (oh there aren't any left

you say   just skins and masks and inconsolable

Tibetans) were it not for   creatures   without

narcissism or fetishes.   Human desire is

avaricious.   Human desire   aspires on wings

says *gather it*   to symmetry   and form   and fear

but here we go again with spectator and voyeur.

Not wanting   to be either   I suppose   I would rather

cling   to a little long-haired   lamb with whom

curl by curl   I could enumerate the forests of the night

burning   more or less unremittingly.

ALONE, RATHER BECAUSE
NOT OTHERWISE

I resemble   myself too much.   In that way I'm
ironic,   or allegorical.

There was the   time you   made a movie of me
I didn't know you were

making--somehow my   presence supposed your
absence, I suppose. So

I was once again   outnumbered. Still gently nursing the
wounds caused by caricature—

sucking the   last sweetness from   the illusion
of idiosyncrasy.   How did that

mouth kiss, I   wonder. How did that   ruined, magenta
hair beguile? In sepia, darling,

like all dream sex: solitude and object-hood a-bountiful.
Your head on the

pillow, fellow. And I,   Señorita Death.

LEADING THE SOLEMN PROCESSION JOYFULLY

after Berryman

Lean me your ear, dear,

while I whistle.

You make a lukewarm wooer.

And grief is too astray for tears. And bleeding—
I'd do it if it would get me anywhere.

You're the touchy one!

Ok then don't notice the straight shape of the
cypress, a damned icon of amazement

that waits to hasten us toward vision or wound.
Just keep moving.

BY SOME STRANGE GLADNESS ELATED

It was a judgeless
day, or a dream
without turbulence or
prediction—

a hummingbird,
too: a needle,
holographic
nightfall. You,
joy boy.

Closed my eyes
in sweet demising.

Not writing.
Not writing.

LED BY THESE SIGNS AND BY THESE INSTANCES

Out my window *a tattooed fragment of turquoise sky* and

yesterday *a red surf incarnadining the beach.*

Not quite enough for a poem, comrades,

yet still the hands type, led on by some lack of

water or nakedness, led on by the stony hair of

dread or the ironic fact that saying something isn't

accomplishing anything at all. It's what I've got to say,

though, that and *light builds skyscrapers on the sea,* and

a mockingbird stopped short right in front of me, then

Shiva came to life in the center of the eucalyptus.

Not much I know but they're things the confused

world hurled at me, while the sun, dying of pleasure,

divided it all into dark matter and hack-work.

FLAME-COLOR MEANS EAST WINDS

In the old days when something used to be at stake
a cusp of wisp meant all music had to run amok.

There was an ethos of neither
when the sun went black.

We gushed and ruminated because crows had
savaged the burlap.

When travelers, interlopers, added frivolity
to the mix the sun, as foretold, came back,
grass breathed,

windows blinked
and I could hear my ancestors calling me--
them for whom I had lowered the windsock

having felt virtuous before under a rare steak sky.

In the old days we dove headfirst into actionless
affection's murky breach.

We sighed into whichever effort
our wanderlust opted for.

There were loaves of bread at the door—
who could have asked for better weather?

THE HERON LEAVES HER HAUNTS IN THE MARSH

Let me go, domestic air, inner conflict and anarchism.
Let me replace

the thick veil of separation
with a thinner veil. The

anchoring point of a marriage is mythical. Catch me
off-guard and slip out for some whiskey

why don't you--

I'm not the one in the leather coat and the
comb-over makeover.

Over me the wind's dumb moan, beside
me the foam and glitter of the Pacific. The

heron has "one of the most begrudging avian takeoffs."

Oh fucking hell I'll go. Have I had a tetanus shot? Not
for years.

HEADLONG FALLS THE SKY IN SHEETS OF RAIN
Topanga Canyon

. . . closing the jungle canyon and its outdoor theater, leaving the actors to improvise only their displacement in space.

No improvisation! says the Haitian woman teaching traditional rituals.

But the actors feel the need to purge themselves: screaming, herding themselves up into a bunch, carrying someone in the air as if he were dead, throwing themselves down on the ground as in pseudo-crisis, singing songs with syllables like ah or la or ooh. All this in the tiny green room.

Grotowski often said that before the real work could be done, a human being would have to vomit out all of these clichés—the "basic human banalities." In other words, improvisation teaches what *not* to do on the stage.

When it stopped raining the actors went to a fish place, where it turned out they had, simultaneously, the same impulse—to jump over the counter and attack the cook. Which they did.

WORK AT YOUR OMINOUS EVENSONG IN VAIN

When Appollinaire was shot in the head after de Chirico had painted a portrait of him with a target on his left temple, artists and poets hailed de Chirico as a prophet.

Omens will always exist—eternal proof of the non-logical in the universe.

> [What omens, then, are the *Superior Petit Beurre* biscuits in *The death of the soul?* (That's obvious—our own dead souls.) What the reclining figure in *Piazza d'Italia?* (Our feet will turn to stone.) What the curious hummingbird looking at me with its tiny eye?]

A phantom stepped into the living room this morning in your old bathrobe—the one your mother gave you. What of that? I say this whole place is gearing up for an epic earthquake.

Look, there's a torso pinned to the side of my house with a black circle where the heart would be. I'm afraid I put it there.

AGAINST THE DARK, LONG TRAILS OF LUMINOUS WHITE

after Samuel Beckett

If I could describe the clouds I would

because today
they're wearing fine white flowing hair against a gunmetal sky.

If I could describe the years
If I could describe the years to you
they'd look like silhouettes of vast shaggy ungulates on short legs
pulling carts of hay against a bright horizon.

But there is no one here no not me either.

(When speaking of myself
when speaking of the sky
when speaking of anything
how can I know
I can't know.)

Where we come from where we go
it annihilates you word by word.

IF ONCE THAT WELL-KNOWN SCENT COMES DOWN THE WIND

The scent of black remnants from the last illegal bonfire on the wind's
invisible hands that are lifting the heads of orange flowers the scent of

whatever it is that climbs out of the dark at daybreak in its thick fur gown
and operatic helmet practicing an old-time eloquence by placing its two knees

playfully on the breast of the meadow if these scents come down the wind
don't go the other way because you see yourself as a city person someone

who has sold off or forgotten the warm zone of forest creatures swaying in
soft focus somewhere in back of the backdrop of severity you've erected

remember the question is not whether sentimental objects do or do not carry
a contagious temporality the question is how to defeat the sterile sexuality of

our excuses while two hawks merge and couple in mid-flight
sunlight sparking off of the attenuated edges of their feathers

AN ANT THAT FEARS
A LEAN OLD AGE

puts grains aside that's a fact but we Charleston-ed backward you and I like
it was New Year's Eve in Moscow 1925 pushing our beaded asses and calves

in platinum behind while trying not to imagine what was coming what terrors
and shames the certain failures of our ember days whether the future would

all grow black or all grow bright (I doze off from time to time with open eyes
but nothing changes) weren't we hoping for something more revolutionary

than that something agit-prop or train track (yet a kind of mnemonic
movement did speak through us as we criss-crossed our attic terrain our

neo-flapper habitat) now that we're asthmatic—heaving like machinery—I
could swear we put the money away somewhere safe and locatable didn't we?

AND IN GREEN MEADOWS RAISE A MARBLE TEMPLE

The sound you hear it's a hammer chiseling time out of fragrance and our
pain it's a pas de deux of childhood dreams and generations' claims it's the

dance of a sand-grain in the stem-crook of a shoreline flame or it's you and
me pulling ourselves along an infinite chain of incongruities toward

unthinkable death (oh tissued scrim of history a skeleton man with a look of
pity asked me up to his apartment the best in New York City) that was long

before we fell into the ayahuasca lord lord and now that we've lost our talent
for impersonating lizards now that we've harvested for ourselves the long

green hair of a river now that we've pawned our ethnic jewelry from Cuzco
and Costco where's the poem that once once held it all for
us all pleasure and

all sense and what is this overintended sandwich of canned meat "boneless,
economical" oh monuments oh polychromatic Kali keeping beat

IN TEMPLES IVORIES WEPT AND BRONZES SWEATED

And we thought we'd invented Dada.
We thought we'd taken begging for money

and booze to a whole new level—
total blues ruination.

Now let's cry through eyes of stone pupil-less.
Or, resuming at the point where we left off, drag

ourselves paralytic through the splendors
of the future—a joy we might otherwise never

have known. Let's then notice a small shiny
key in the keyhole. Let's then argue whether

chance is an accident
or an attribute of destiny.

HIS EYES ABLAZE WITH SEA-GREEN LIGHT

So much said and done. So much sadness and
doing. He called home often. He ate and drank,

cooked, wrote books, had years ago broken the
code of animal language and so talked

to cats and horses—the rest, he said, didn't
have so much to say. We went aground

many times—and talked about dying. We shared
what might be called an honesty bred by poverty

(he was her never-weaned though not her favored
child). One day we raised our eyelids and were

older. One day the mysteriously reappearing
semi-truck of his dreams overturned and all

its liberated penguins tottered back to
Kangaroo Island. He'd known all along that they would.

What is yesterday/What is tomorrow?
Which are we moving toward? Sometimes I think,

like Orpheus, we're halting on the very brink
of light and looking back. Other times

I think we're done with pentameter and grieving.

LIGHT CHAFF AND FALLING LEAVES
OR A PAIR OF FEATHERS

on the ground can spook a horse who won't flinch when faced
with a backhoe or a pack of Harleys. I call it "horse

ophthalmology," because it is a different kind of system—
not celestial, necessarily, but vision in which the small,

the wispy, the lightly lifted or stirring threads of existence
excite more fear than louder and larger bodies do. It's Matthew

who said that the light of the body is the eye, and that if
the eye is healthy the whole body will be full of light. Maybe

in this case "light" can also mean "lightness." With my eyes of
corrupted and corruptible flesh I'm afraid I see mostly darkness

by which I mean heaviness. How great is that darkness? Not
as great as the inner weightlessness of horses whose eyes perceive,

correctly I believe, the threat of annihilation in every wind-blown
dust mote of malignant life. All these years I've been watching

out warily in obvious places (in bars, in wars, in night cities and
nightmares, on furious seas). Yet what's been trying to destroy

me has lain hidden inside friendly-seeming breezes, behind
soft music, beneath the carpet of small things one can barely see.

The eye is also a lamp, says Matthew, a giver of light, bestower
of incandescent honey, which I will pour more cautiously

over the causeways I travel from now on. What's that whisper?
Just the delicate sweeping away of somebody's life.

DRAWN BY A TEAM OF THREE-LEGGED FISH-TAILED HORSES

The road to death is crooked, even for a god. Your
three-legged fish-tailed horses never want to pull in the

same direction so the chariot lurches and jerks forward
in a confused motion, driving the charioteer to curse, to

use the whip, sometimes to crash against crusty underwater
cliffs or plummet into sudden drop-offs in the sea floor.

How much more difficult for poor humans caught between
the names of things and the iridescences of perceptions—

one minute walking alone and in love on a mountain path,
the next waking up on a clinic's cot face to face with

different pastures—out of this moment something suddenly
expressing itself in a poem, and out of that moment another

plummeting. Meanwhile herds of shapeless enormous seals
hover in the sea above hidden flowerbeds. I live in a kind of

lurching and jerking amid shimmers, glimpses, and recognitions,
between the day and its passing. Last night I stood beneath

a coral tree whose black branches were full of snowy egrets
squawking and shifting before settling down for sleep. It was

a picture for a Roman tapestry! Almost an image for a poem! And then I felt another plummeting. It had something to do

with beauty; something to do with the dogged willfulness of specificity and its opposite, all the alienated noncommittal

wavering of the sea. The beautiful sea. What could be more unbreakable?

DAYS SUCH AS THESE SHONE OUT AND WENT THEIR WAY

*It is the organization of these images that structures
the space within which our freedom asserts itself.*
Alain Robbe-Grillet

On the ploughed earth sits   an earth-brown person
wrapped in red and with a   tranquil expression devoting
herself to the taste and   consumption of a plant.

Roots are coming out of her shoes.   They grow out of
her clothing, on her wrists, the   folds of her sleeves, her
hips, and even the little box   lying on the ground next to

her has a thin blue root   cheekily stretching toward soil.
In this painting, which hangs   over the bar in one of my
favorite hotels in Oaxaca   the woman's belly seems to be

illuminated in the form of an   onion. Light-bulb/plant
bulb; when I'm lit as it were   I find this image hysterically
and stupidly germane.   A week ago I was drinking in a

different bar with a friend.   We ate mussels, and I imagined
us, Gail and Jaz, sprayed by   waves on a rocky breakwater—
these black and nacre shells   hunching in sunlight—far

far away from the calculations of   relationships and the cerebral
universe of signs. Above us   a painting depicted a chaotic,
bursting landscape in which   hands grew out of the ground

armed with knives. A floating   body, maybe Icarus, maybe
his sister, detonated into startling   flames. (Undoubtedly
these images have a   hidden rapport that would

require a lengthier conversation.)   Marriages blow up
or last. Embryonic   children become something
other than our puppets.   What's always tricky

is knowing when to read for   metaphor and when to
let the days shine out and go   their way. On a road outside
my house, an indefatigable   automobile refuses to ignite.

Inside, a corridor leads   to a great wooden staircase
upon which an amused nude   lies in an almost cubist sprawl.

LET NOT THE SPANGLED LIZARD'S SCALY BACK

distract you while you scale these boulders

or you'll miss the otherworldly doe and young
fawn picking their way through the ragged

archipelago of rocks toward Big Bear Lake with
its soft rim of marsh and burnt cedar not to

mention the moon hanging rather outrageously
low in the daytime sky I miss them

routinely because I'm watching a
bee war sometimes because I've been standing

in the funerary line of humanity too
long breathing solemn fog onto the face of

some humbling mirror none of this stops the
sky from continuing none of it explains the flashing

turbulence of serpent beside the path or
the bewildering shoal of blue wings above I wish

that my thoughts could be projected like light
thrown as if they were rays of light all over this

landscape would that constitute a reconciliation
or betrayal of all these differentiations

in all seriousness if I try to picture my thoughts
they look like souls in Botticelli's Hell like flames

some of them with buds of miniscule human faces
which is also what they look like in Paradise

IN THESE LATITUDES OF INDETERMINATE WAVES

Stéphane Mallarmé

these oaks mark time in the tempo of centuries
one by my deck having taken twenty years to notice
I'd moved in next to it

every day with involuntary simultaneous
exhalations a brief exchange of our equally distinctive
aromas we say good morning before

going about our different yet proximate lives
bird-time is something more difficult to rhythm into
what with migration and wings

PITCH-PINES OR GUILTY YEWS
OR DARK GREEN IVY

These will make your soil black and you might then
mistake it for rich soil soil in which anything could

grow and you could feed a whole nation of people
with it but not if the blackness comes from one of

these then you're finished then you're washed up
as a farmer you may as well turn Platonic

philosopher and look death in the mirror
permanently and seriously make dust

your paper so to speak (just don't blame it on my
oak tree she had nothing to do with your soil!)

but time is flying flying beyond memory and now
you want to know why God gave you such a raw

deal with the fake rich dirt and all kind of a "dirty"
trick not what you bargained for beautiful in its

way of course though where does that weird optimism
come from the way each of us at first believes

that we won't be the ones robbed of life by
some disease or accident and let's face it we are precisely

those so put a little pluck and wisdom in it and sing it
with feeling sing it as if you were Sarasvati in a windstorm

and no one were guilty there were no such poisons
and ravenous black vines weren't rising in the night

THROUGH THE LIQUID AIR
OF SUMMER

UCLA radio-oncology

This smiling dust of words
falling on appalling t-shirts

Really it's anathema
to be there so
I'll speak of it when I speak no more

I'll speak of you
fatally leaning toward expressiveness

just like one of the living

it's not a trial by fire it's by fluorescence
in which light it's hard to ferret out
any endlessness

a tiled wide path leading behind us
a blue-ish buzzing of pure white bees
ahead

we exit through an unsubtle door into
maddeningly charitable sunlight

NEW TREATMENTS
MADE THINGS WORSE

an elegy

There were no baby elephant gods to be found
in the philodendron. She could've cared less.

To her mind it was all non-immanent—there was
nothing to anticipate—it would go on as it had gone—

always a subject, always some selfhood stalking an
object, killing it, dressing it up, consuming it, all just

sowing and reaping (not, as I sometimes like to say,
stewing, weeping). "A banal project," she called it, life.

But she lit the votive candles to make me happy,
with closed eyelids, silently appreciating the privacy

I sometimes allowed her. I knew her well—had
memorized, even, her arms, stained over the years

by the yellow-gray smoke of her chemistry experiments.
Often she dreamed that tiny hands were patting her

everywhere —tiny disembodied hands were braiding
her hair while she slept—chubby angel-hands

were flying away with her soul. She rejected all of my
attempts to translate these images. "Isolate flecks"

was a phrase she liked, from a William Carlos Williams
poem. She saw everything as an isolated fleck and

hated the way people were always trying to bring flecks
together into coherent systems---like me and my Ganesh

project. We never found him, with his palliative phallic
trunk, rolling roundly and peacefully on my plant leaves

the way I'd asked for him to appear. I wish he had, just
once. It would have been something, in addition to death,

she could not have finessed so easily into insignificance.

WILD OLIVES, BITTER-LEAVED, ALONE SURVIVE

Past the time of repast and the time of fasting
and the time of everyone going away, going back

to widowhood (yours the pang, but his the undiminished,
undecaying gladness),

nothing to be done
but cart the suits off to Salvation Army, revise

the narrative—not what you had to say, always,
but a colder assessment: he never really had it in him

to be great. He was lazy. Never thought things through
to the bottom, always half-grasping, sweeping by, ideas

spiraling up like ornate staircases into nowhere.
Should've died earlier. You say this to his shadow

arguing on your walks about who loved whom more fully,
whose happiness had depth, what has lasted.

Men "give their lives" they say, and women "give life"
and it all feels something like living inside someone else's

body, and then he dies and all that is ended, and
the usual remedy is to go and enter other lives (although

I just wrote "lies").

LET THOUGHT BECOME YOUR BEAUTIFUL LOVER

For then thought will be as noiseless as a mellowing pear, or it will lope out like a wind-wild unbridled horse, or pause with you on your balcony,

taking in the sea smell, not hearing the words of the poet saying love is an ornate piano, love is a seismic pulse, love is never anything a poet says it is.

It will be as enchanting as a wandering orphic singer in her little boat surrounded by attentive birds. Indeed, were I not now furling my sails and

hastening to turn my prow toward land, I might hold forth further on the topic. And you might think me beautiful.

WHAT IS IT THAT SLOWS THE LINGERING DUSK

As I lift my face a thick dew settles on it. On top of that wind scatters grains of silver sand that flicker like stars so that my face becomes a small reflection of the sky facing the real sky, suggesting a possibility of infinite correspondence and depth, of an undifferentiated cosmos in which I am not I but am everything. Like all intimations of immortality this takes only a minute. After that I drink a luminous beer and shoo a blackbird from my Japanese maple. Black feathers fall through scarlet leaves inside a glow from window light. And then there's the insect panic, and a great ocean wave rearing up in the mania of midnight, some bothersome recriminations from a rustled curtain, a cup of subtle tea, decisions to be made about the newly arrived fleet of small lapis carvings . . .

AND THE WILD WILLOW-BED
DEMANDS ATTENTION

There was a wedding on our street—
a girl named Oats married a man named Wheat.

Pursuing is pleasure and parting is grief.
And parting is parting forever.

Don't turn a deaf leaf!
I've seen the whip-like vines flash green

insinuations while I sweep.
Oh muddy gardening shoes!

Oh lacerations from the blades of mournful
sheaves! So much for bales and wreaths—

we wed and die because the wild willow-bed
demands it. Don't ask why.

HOW LUCKY, IF THEY KNOW THEIR HAPPINESS

after Cesar Aira

The problem with ghosts is that they never really want to go anywhere; they won't do the wave; and I always underestimate the intensity of their addictions to drafty places and period dress.

Also they say things like:

Not words and pictures but poems.

Not poems about pictures but pictures.

Not work but words and breathing windows.

We had an art opening in the old lodge. We planned to flood the orangery with riddles. We wanted both figures and flickering, but then it rained all night, drowning out everything but the ghosts of these ideas. (The chandelier alone, catching a few drops of rainy light, was vivid.) Now I find myself looking for a tool with which I might slice the morning into equal parts of vinyl and lichen. Because they told me to.

Also they said:

All you think about is sex.

There you go again, talking about Paris.

That time there were only two of them. One smelled like money.

DOLPHINS ARE
PEOPLE TOO

Before Marlena strung crystals and mirrors in our trees
so that when the wind blew crazy light flashed off in all

directions, before Peter made a song bow out of locust
wood and played it against his head which worked like a

sounding box when he hit the bow's one string with his
pocket knife, before the mean old macaroon-maker was

kicked out of hell, before no one answered the question,
before Topanga meant Mountains to the Ocean, before

dark clouds rose in the south, before Galileo looked
through the peephole, before somebody took my sister's

fa-sol-la and made it a nightmare, before any man loved
a woman, before the comandante went to jail, before

Dan put the salt and pepper in his poetry which before
that had had a lot to say about trains coming or trains

going or people getting on and off of trains, before tweed
jacket boredom, October, gunfire, Nigeria, or 1966,

before the wildest hour shook its violet mane out all over
the evening mountains, before the car horn and the barking

dog and the homeless guy playing flute in the lot next to
Moon's Market, before fat cows and robbed graves, before

Mozart, before glitter showered down on the disco floor
like the promise of enduring love, before you wanted

anything, before the hunter Actaeon saw the goddess Diana
bathing naked in the lake for which transgression she made him

a stag, before the stag was chased down and dismembered
by dogs he had until that minute owned, before faster was

not necessarily better, before Cleopatra met Julius Caesar,
Mark Antony, *or* death, before the baby swallowed the tiny

corner of window pane, before Santa Ana winds sliced in
through the kitchen window, before Crazy Horse had his

crazy horse dream, before coffee filters, Kafka, slavery,
Sweet Georgia Brown, and the *Mahabarata*, they all said the

heck with it and walked into the Pacific, their arms
disappearing, their hands slanting off into fins.

MIRACULOUSLY PREGNANT
BY THE WIND

Like Virgil's mares who *conquer mountain steeps and swim through rivers/ Soon as the flame of lust catches their vitals* I stand on a high cliff and turn my face toward Zephyr.

It's after idylls, after all, and
the interior censors have already shaken their fingers--

as if an overcooked oyster somehow secreted a pearl on their plate—
it's embarrassing, or worse, it's vulgar, and yet
horse-madness stirs even in those of us no longer

capable of dropping handkerchiefs or babies, those of us
stopping on a bluff to sniff the air in springtime. Such
flowering and restlessness. But face it, I may have had the best
already. Sustained exquisite polymorphous agitation—

everything wind-lit to the point of guaranteed transmigration.

EVEN GIRLS SPINNING THEIR NIGHTLY STINT OF WOOL

after a car crash

   I liked the idea
that I was dead

   quintessentially abstract
my surroundings an eternity

of pale blue
                    as if God
were as wary of images
or as wary of
narrative

as I am
   (it gives the impression we're

experiencing
something   navigable

 or worse that we are moving
     irreversibly
              from birth to
death)

  I like to think
       occasionally one
                    slips

  through a kind
of synchronic   gap

        the beam of a headlight
seen

through a parted
    curtain of broken glass
                          even
those girls
     spinning their
           nightly stint

of wool can
          dream of this

KAMIKAZE FEMINIST FISH

That time is past/And all its aching joys
are now no more,/And all its dizzy raptures.
William Wordsworth

And then the goldfish, whose bowl had been placed mistakenly on the radiator, leapt shimmering out of the water, landing on a heap of old Ms. magazines piled on an end table next to them.

Wow, writes the poet, a woman in her twenties whose life has not yet really organized itself, *those fish! They're just like me—bravely ideological, flashing their gaudy appendages awkwardly and proud beyond the no longer habitable waters of captivity . . .*

A woman discovering this journal in a desk drawer after thirty-some years writes in her own journal, *I'm not just this person, full of regret and self-doubt, who writes right now—I am also one who has written—one for whom the whole world once winked and signed.*

(The fantasy of authenticity is sublime, isn't it? The farmhouse outside Siena retaining a couple of original stones in its entryway; the expensive Moroccan chair "once carried on the back of a camel.")

FAR BE IT FROM ME TO INDULGE IN A NAP

There's so much to do for example
we could release feathered

dragons lyre birds and the genius phoenix from their underground dungeons
unclothe the lewd and goose-fleshed muses breathe the clear atoms of

fearless

hours put on absurd flippers if we want or not do any of that and just sit
practicing to die Tibetan monks do it they say you can get really good at it

here I am
looking at the bright side again

bright as a bird's eye in the black tunnel between leaves
bright as money in the bank
bird thou never wert

THEN ARE WILD THICKETS
LOUD WITH SINGING BIRDS

What woman, asks Hélène Cixous, hasn't accused herself
of being a monster. Or been accused, I would emphasize.

Our desires are monstrous. Our power is monstrous.
Therefore we should, and do for the most part, hide. But

when dawn comes, we can't repress ourselves. The world
must be woken! It's a startling gift, to have one's obligation—

rousing the house—and one's joy so utterly intermixed—
perhaps today I *won't* go to the writing table and put to paper

that simple and profound poem of death I always imagine
leaving behind for my friends.

We're such infinite, ebullient birds, ladies. Such humorous
aliens. And we have joyful, well-intentioned,

and inclusive news: it's day! (God how wrong they all are
about us . . .) Wake up! It's another fatherfucking day!

WHAT NEED TO TELL OF AUTUMN'S STORMS AND STARS

It can hit you hard as a whip of grainy dust blown in
your eyes the realization that you need to tell someone

all of it even the worst in words not cheapened with showy
sound effects and with or without the dismembering con-

ventions of allegory—that you need to write about this woodpile
glowing between us like a dragon's hoard of gold-plated

bones—do more than to sit in the dust eating spiders and crust
whether or not you'll be taken for mad and if you are

taken for mad at least you'll be left alone. What can I tell you
about the evils of other people except that often I've found

human interaction to be a ferocious and almost feral feasting
not unlike the one Dante finds in which Count Ugolino

eternally feeds on the uncooked flesh of his son afterwards
wiping his mouth with the hair of the man he has just eaten.

Now that I've covered that let's step out into the autumn evening
and happily—perhaps drows'd with the fume of poppies—look up

because the dim lit sky is almost drooling with our dying
hence our wind-swept laments of gratitude and longing

SELECTIVELY, USING YOUR FINGERNAILS

Try to focus your attention behind your
own reflection and onto the minute bio-optical lenses inside your eyes—

those infinitesimal portals hard as rice grains glowing like opals with
inexplicable interior incandescence.

One caveat; after you do
there'll be no more galloping off toward the beautiful shore, you get my

meaning, no mist meets mist in the drunken cubist nights of La
Habra, no poetic gestures left for you at all in fact but scratching

out all traces of this insight, this self-recognition.

What did you think it would be this life all dining on violets and
intravenous moonbeams?

Look—after leaving its fingerprints on the walls of my house
a shadow has landed in the grove, bent like an elbow

and wearing a long, blue, formal, mourning glove.

THE TREES THAT LIFT THEMSELVES SPONTANEOUSLY

The day's just handed me a glass-bulb pipe and an
energy drink despite my death-fetish. Now that

we've met, you can see I'm haunted by meaning and
both excited by and worried about the possibility that

writing is moving more deeply into graphic regions
such as actual figuration. I'm already quite aware

of the con game that is rhetoric but frankly I suck at
drawing, so how if that happens will I ever even start

to assert real authority in the life of my people? Oh
aleph-bet. And now the preverbal seagulls of San Pedro

cry by, above high-reaching greenery. I had nothing
to do with their rising, or with the trees meeting

united like lovers in the sky. The wind spins as quietly
as smoke here. I'm the woman filming it.

OR RAIN OF ACORNS FROM A SHAKEN OAK

The door opened. The door went on opening.
Your eyelashes were like the rays around the star

in the middle of a shot-out windowpane. The violinists
had lifted their bows . . .

Let's face it, we're deserters, you and I,
in the "armies of the upright." For us, simple

and honest declarations are the most difficult
thing to attempt or arrive at. (Those who've stepped

off that cliff have been found on the riverbank
completely naked, stripped of their jewelry, their

lace-up boots, sometimes even in groups with river
mud packed beneath their eyelids.)

So let's shake this poem of an oak tree again, as if
loving were as much about passing the time

(gathering acorns) as it is about time passing (the
oak tree growing). We who are stationed outside cast

elaborate shadows on the grass. Trees, and the years, and
far off, distant laughter. Do we love each other?

I think the lyric form requires it.

WHEN IT'S BONE-HARD UNDER A NORTH WIND

plough not an unknown pain. Now is not the time
to question those things we're
always stopping to think about. For example,

we're always envying the ability of fire
to reduce things. Then, in the novel, the beetle-shaped
men come with their epees;

a chair falls over and a tiger leaps;

someone cries with conviction, "No, it's all too small!"

And now I feel apprehensive about future intensities and
hurting. Must I give up fathoming

the depths of life?
The sky is bone-hard.

Wind issuing from someplace not from here.

THE BANK ALL GREEN WITH CELERY, THE CUCUMBER SNAKING

Thus I, too, come to the

world, Mrs. Dalloway (the world
in which trees drag their leaves
like nets through depths of air),

bearing flowers. And what of the
void? Today a hot wind of dust,
sandalwood, and musk is blowing

from the land of the dead. Moot
though it seems here in the idyllic
world, the emerald creek-side where

I epiphanize. In my own quaint way
I like living, I say, as my body, of its
own accord, pushes forth a parsimonious,

vegetal frill.

A SPACIOUS CAVE
MUCH VISITED BY WAVES

Don't look directly at the mad old
bitch stitching a sheet of lime silk at a red lacquer table

inside the cave. Stitching what?
A line of poetry perhaps.
Something new and wise, meticulous, and sufficient

to outlast the treacherously serene days of immortality. A
thin but impenetrable scrim separates us from her. The green sea

heaves mightily against it. There are white rats gnashing
their teeth and some unidentifiable demons

exploding into weeping. *All the girls who wrote poetry
are dead,* they cry. An earthquake is rumbling somewhere

nearby. A bright new fabulous yellow day is almost arising.

WE OFFER REEKING ENTRAILS
TO THE GODS
sitting with Jerry Stahl at Mimosa Café

Then there's the treacherous mystery of Tina who had her breasts removed because the weight of them felt like death to her. But they're only tender pitchers of milk, I said, at which remark her parrot laughed, imitating my self-conscious chuckle. When Tina lit a crack pipe, Stephanie, another local, said, Now you're sucking the devil's horn, to which she replied, sometimes a crack pipe is only a crack pipe. The parrot laughed my very distinctive laugh again. Do you prefer angel horns, Tina asked, for which none of us had an answer. So she left with her bird and a herd of goats—all employees of a local landscaping business.

AND THE OWL ON THE ROOFTOP
WATCHING THE SUN GO DOWN

The day came down to nothing and of the nothing
there is very little left. *Too whit too whoo.*

*

The vocalized sound haunted by meaning as if by an
incurable illness. Face like white frost, expressionless

*

so that the dead have nothing to go by. No
rainbows stooping over for a drink. No ravens crying
thickly "rain, rain." Night is the ink-play of God the
literati-artist. And it is

*

an apt maneuver, as false as it is true. The
masked and the exposed? I see them both coming.
Strange horns and motorcycle engines? *Too whit*

*

too whoo. Sun, you're wearing feathers like a lady bright.
Gap craving night. Wide enough to decline through.

NOTES AND ACKNOWLEDGMENTS

The title of almost every poem in this book is a line taken from *The Georgics* by Virgil, L. P. Wilkinson translator. The quoted line in "Miraculously pregnant by the wind" is also taken from *The Georgics*.

Quoted lines in "And the wild willow-bed demands attention" are taken from an anonymous American roots song.

In "A Spacious cave much visited by waves" the quoted line is taken from Roberto Bolaño's *Distant Star*.

The quoted phrase in "Or rain of acorns from a shaken oak" is Virginia Woolf's.

*

Grateful acknowledgement to the editors of the following publications in which these poems first appeared, sometimes in different versions.

A Poetry Congeries "Let thought become your beautiful lover," "Drawn by a team of three-legged fish-tailed horses," "Wild beasts and fish, cattle and colored birds"

Askew "Dolphins are People Too," "Neither can every soil bear everything"

Calyx: A Journal of Women and the Arts "Wild olives, bitter-leaved, alone survive"

Catamaran "Let not the spangled lizard's scaly back"

Chicago Quarterly Review "The light and shade upon the globe," "For not in vain we name the constellations"

Denver Quarterly "in these latitudes/of indeterminate/waves"

Dusie "By some strange gladness elated"

Fiction Week "New treatments made things worse"

The Offending Adam "Dry cracking sounds are heard," "An acre or two of land that no one wanted," "An ant that fears a lean old age," "How lucky, if they know their happiness"

Poetry "Light chaff and falling leaves or a pair of feathers"

Poetry International "And mend the wreckage of a ruined home"

Pool "Let thought become your beautiful lover," "Kamikaze Feminist Fish"

Spillway "Days such as these shone out and went their way"

Teesta Rangi (India) "Clearer than amber gliding over stones"

Yew Journal. "Against the dark, long trails of luminous white," "And in green meadows rains a marble temple," "In temples ivories wept and bronzes sweated," "Far be it from me to indulge in a nap"

And to the editors of the anthology *The Coiled Serpent* (Tia Chucha Press) in which the poems "Dolphins are People Too" and "And in green meadows raise a marble temple" appear.

*

Many thanks and much love to Shark, and to Karen Kevorkian, Molly Bendall, Alicia Partnoy, Sarah Maclay, David St. John, James Cushing, Diane Seuss, Daniel Tiffany, Judith Taylor, Danny Baker, Antonio Leiva, Ash Good, and everyone at What Books Press.

GAIL WRONSKY is the author, coauthor, or translator of twelve books of poetry and prose. She is the recipient of an Artists Fellowship from the California Arts Council and has been a finalist for the Western Arts Federation Poetry Prize. Alicia Partnoy's book *Fuegos Florales (Flowering Fires)*, with her translations, recently won the American Poetry Prize from Settlement House Press. Her poems, reviews, and essays appear widely in journals and anthologies. She teaches poetry and women's writing at Loyola Marymount University in Los Angeles, and lives in Topanga Canyon.

LOS ANGELES

TITLES FROM
WHAT BOOKS PRESS

POETRY

Molly Bendall & Gail Wronsky, *Bling & Fringe (The L.A. Poems)*

Laurie Blauner, *It Looks Worse Than I Am*

Kevin Cantwell, *One of Those Russian Novels*

Ramón García, *Other Countries*

Karen Kevorkian, *Lizard Dream*

Holaday Mason & Sarah Maclay, *The "She" Series: A Venice Correspondence*

Carolie Parker, *Mirage Industry*

Patty Seyburn, *Perfecta*

Judith Taylor, *Sex Libris*

Lynne Thompson, *Start with a Small Guitar*

Gail Wronsky, *Imperfect Pastorals*

Gail Wronsky, *So Quick Bright Things*
BILINGUAL, SPANISH TRANSLATED BY ALICIA PARTNOY

ART

Gronk, *A Giant Claw*
BILINGUAL, SPANISH

Chuck Rosenthal, Gail Wronsky & Gronk,
Tomorrow You'll Be One of Us: Sci Fi Poems

PROSE

Rebbecca Brown, *They Become Her*

François Camoin, *April, May, and So On*

A.W. DeAnnuntis, *Master Siger's Dream*

A.W. DeAnnuntis, *The Final Death of Rock and Roll and Other Stories*

A.W. DeAnnuntis, *The Mermaid at the Americana Arms Motel*

A.W. DeAnnuntis, *The Mysterious Islands and Other Stories*

Katharine Haake, *The Origin of Stars and Other Stories*

Katharine Haake, *The Time of Quarantine*

Mona Houghton, *Frottage & Even As We Speak: Two Novellas*

Rich Ives, *The Balloon Containing the Water Containing the Narrative Begins Leaking*

Annette Leddy, *Earth Still*

Rod Val Moore, *Brittle Star*

Chuck Rosenthal, *Are We Not There Yet? Travels in Nepal, North India, and Bhutan*

Chuck Rosenthal, *Coyote O'Donohughe's History of Texas*

Chuck Rosenthal, *West of Eden: A Life in 21st Century Los Angeles*

Chuck Rosenthal & Gail Wronsky, *The Shortest Farewells are the Best*

Forrest Roth, *Gary Oldman Is a Building You Must Walk Through*

Jessica Sequeira, *Rhombus and Oval*

What Books Press books may be ordered from:
SPDBOOKS.ORG | ORDERS@SPDBOOKS.ORG | (800) 869 7553 | AMAZON.COM

Visit our website at
WHATBOOKSPRESS.COM

www.ingramcontent.com/pod-product-compliance
Lightning Source LLC
Chambersburg PA
CBHW030236100526
44584CB00015BB/1543